the Garfield Gallery 3

Jim Davis

HODDER AND STOUGHTON
LONDON   SYDNEY   AUCKLAND   TORONTO

GARFIELD DESIGNS

The fifteen GARFIELD illustrations within this book have been reproduced from posters by kind permission of the manufacturers:

Argus Communications

Argus Communications distribute a wide range of GARFIELD merchandise which includes:

Posters · Greeting Cards · Postcards
Stationery · Calendars · Diaries
Giftwrap & Tags · Clothing · Badges
Fun Accessories · Stickers

These products are available from most leading greeting card shops, stationers and department stores. For further information why not contact Argus direct at:
Customer Enquiries
Argus Communications, DLM House,
Edinburgh Way, Harlow, Essex CM20 2HL
Tel (0279) 39441

British Library Cataloguing in Publication Data

Davis, Jim, *1945 –*
   The Garfield gallery.
   3
   I. Title
   741.5'973   PN6728.G2

   ISBN 0-340-38152-3

First published in Great Britain 1985
Second impression 1986

Published by Hodder and Stoughton Children's Books, a division of Hodder and Stoughton Ltd, Mill Road, Dunton Green, Sevenoaks, Kent TN13 2YJ

Printed in Italy by New Interlitho S.p.A., Milan

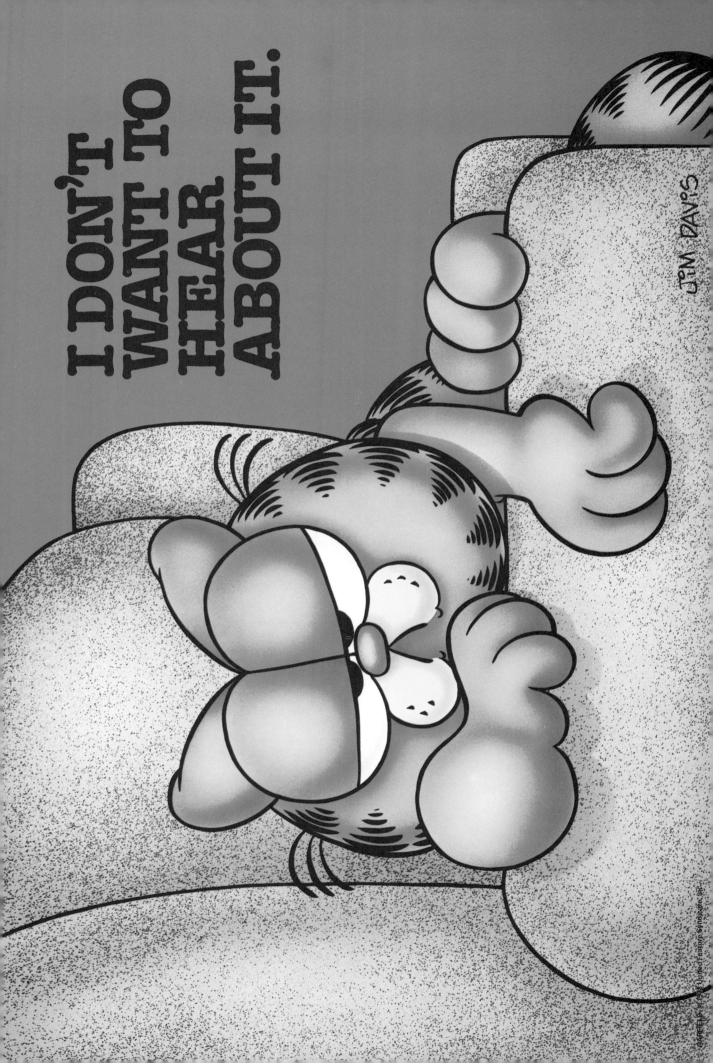

The material things in life aren't important to me, but I do like the stuff

JIM DAVIS

© 1984 United Feature Syndicate, Inc.

7-8   JIM DAVIS

Some things just aren't meant to be

YAWN

IT'S BEDDY-BYE TIME AGAIN

TONIGHT I THINK I'LL TAKE A DEEP BREATH, SLOWLY CLOSE MY EYES AND SAVOR THE HEAVY FEELING OF SLEEP GRADUALLY OVERTAKING MY BODY

PAT! PAT! PAT!

THEN AGAIN IT WOULD BE FUN TO HAVE A CUP OF COFFEE AND TOSS AND TURN FOR A COUPLE OF HOURS, THEN SLEEP 'TIL NOON

OR MAYBE I'LL RUN AROUND THE BLOCK, COLLAPSE INTO BED EXHAUSTED AND FALL ASLEEP INSTANTLY

OR I COULD WATCH THE ALL-NIGHT MOVIES ON TV UNTIL MY EYELIDS GET SO HEAVY I COULDN'T POSSIBLY HOLD THEM OPEN ANY LONGER

SIGH... SO MUCH SLEEPING TO DO AND SO FEW NIGHTS

JIM DAVIS

6-24

The spirit is willing but the flesh is weak!

N

JIM DAVIS

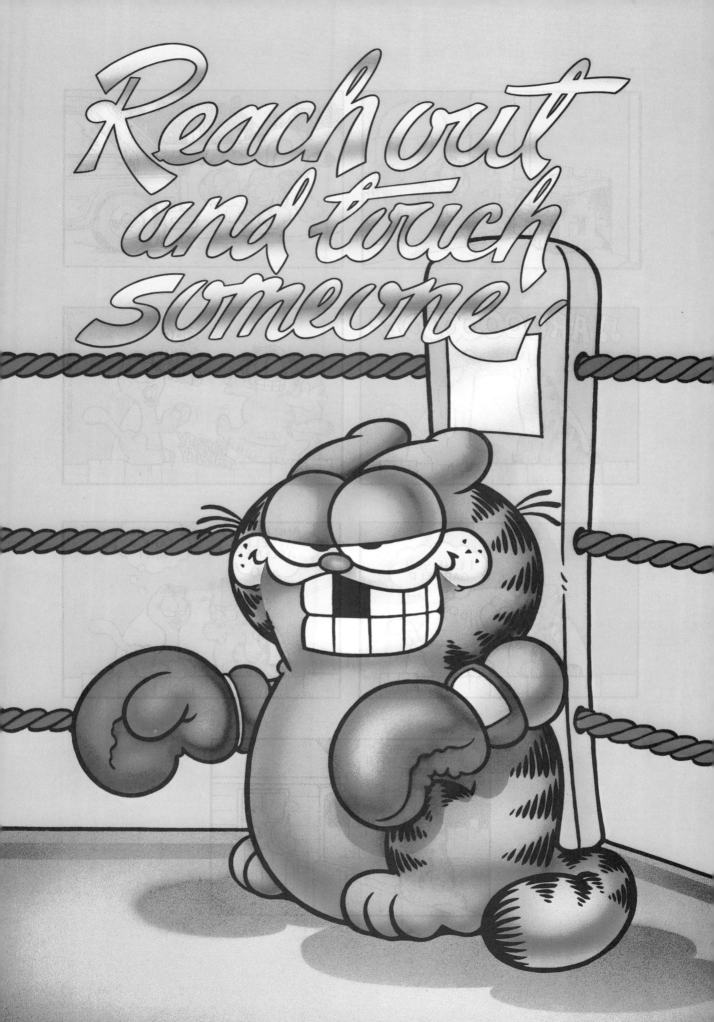

JIM DAVIS

FETCH THE
STICK, ODIE!

5-13

JIM DAVIS